LESSONS FROM
POPE FRANCIS
FOR CHILDREN

BY ANGELA M. BURRIN

ILLUSTRATED BY MARIA CRISTINA LO CASCIO

The First Pope

Do you remember St. Peter? He was one of Jesus' apostles. Jesus had a great plan for Peter's life. One day Jesus said to Peter, "You are Peter, and upon this rock I will build my church."

After Jesus rose from the dead, Peter was filled with the Holy Spirit and began sharing the good news of Jesus' life, death, and resurrection with everyone he met. Just as Jesus said, Peter became the leader of the church. Peter went to Rome and was eventually martyred there. He is buried underneath St. Peter's Basilica in Vatican City.

There have been many popes since St. Peter. Pope Francis, who is a successor of St. Peter, was elected Pope on March 13, 2013. Perhaps you remember when the white smoke appeared out of the chimney at the Vatican in Rome? When Pope Francis came out to greet all the people gathered in St. Peter's Square, he asked them, "Please pray for me." So why don't you stop right now and ask the Holy Spirit to help Pope Francis with all of his responsibilities as the head of the Catholic Church.

Pope Francis spends a lot of time speaking about how we can love Jesus and one another more. Did you know that Pope Francis tweets? Perhaps you can ask your parents to show you some of them!

In the following pages, you can learn some important lessons from Pope Francis. So please turn to the next page and let's begin!

"God's Love for Us Is So Great!"

One day a very special messenger came to the home of a young girl named Mary. The messenger was the angel Gabriel. "Mary, don't be afraid!" he said. "Your heavenly Father is pleased with you. You are to give birth to a son, and you are to name him Jesus." Mary asked, "How will this happen?" The angel said, "The Holy Spirit will come upon you. The baby will be called holy, Son of the Most High." Mary replied, "I am the Lord's servant! Let it happen as you say."

Why do you think your heavenly Father wanted his only Son Jesus to be born into the world? Because he loves you and he wants you to spend eternity with him in heaven. Pope Francis often tells us how much our heavenly Father loves us. Here is your first lesson from Pope Francis:

God's love for us is so great, so deep. It is an unfailing love, one which always takes us by the hand and supports us, lifts us up, and leads us on... God does not forget about us, any of us! He loves us, and does not forget about us.

Think about Jesus taking your hand. He walks beside you everywhere— at home, at school, at sports events, at church—everywhere! You are very precious and important to your heavenly Father. He gave you the gift of life because he loves you.

Pope Francis wants me to know that God loves me!

"We Are All Called to Be Friends with Jesus"

Zacchaeus wanted to see Jesus when he came walking through his hometown of Jericho. But he had two problems. He was so short that he couldn't see Jesus over the crowds. And he was an unpopular tax collector. He often cheated people by making them pay more taxes and keeping the extra money for himself. Zacchaeus knew people didn't want to be near him.

So Zacchaeus spied a sycamore tree and decided to climb it. Suddenly, Jesus stopped and looked up at him and said, "Zacchaeus, I must stay at your house today." On the way back to his home, Zacchaeus told Jesus, "I will share my money with the poor and I will pay back four times those I have cheated." That day Zacchaeus began a special friendship with Jesus.

We are all called to be friends with Jesus… Let Jesus also call us by name! In the depths of our hearts, let us listen to his voice which says, "Today I must stop at your house," that is, in your heart, in your life.

Jesus wants to be your friend! Take a few minutes now to talk to Jesus. Thank him for wanting to be most important person in your life. Invite him to come to your "house"—which is your heart—and tell Jesus that you love him.

Pope Francis wants me to invite Jesus to be my friend!

"Holy Spirit, Make My Heart Open"

Ten days after Jesus had ascended into heaven, the disciples and Jesus' mother, Mary, were in the upper room in Jerusalem. The doors were locked because the disciples were afraid. While they were praying, they suddenly heard a loud noise that sounded like a strong wind. Then they saw flames of fire over their heads. "It's the Holy Spirit!" they said. "Jesus has kept his promise!"

Once the disciples received the Holy Spirit, they did amazing things. Peter and the other disciples went out into the streets and told everyone about Jesus. The crowds heard what they were saying, each in their own language. The disciples healed people in the name of Jesus. The Holy Spirit also helped them to love everyone, even those who were of a different religion or from a foreign country.

Pope Francis wants to teach you about the gift of the Holy Spirit:

Let us open the doors to the Holy Spirit… How beautiful it would be if each of you, every evening, could say, "Today at school, at home, at work, guided by God, I showed a sign of love towards one of my friends, my parents, an older person! How beautiful."

Pope Francis has also given you a prayer to the Holy Spirit:

"Holy Spirit, make my heart open to the word of God; make my heart open to goodness; make my heart open to the beauty of God every day."

Pope Francis wants me to open my heart to the Holy Spirit!

"God Never Tires of Forgiving You"

Jesus wanted the people to know that their heavenly Father forgives all their sins, so he told them a parable. The younger son of a rich man was bored. He asked his father for his share of his inheritance and left home. The son did many wrong things and spent all of his money. He got a job working for a farmer, and when he was hungry, he ate the pigs' food.

Then the son decided to return and ask for his father's forgiveness. As he got near his home, his father saw him and ran to him. The father was so happy that he threw a big party to celebrate! In this lesson, Pope Francis has some great thoughts about our heavenly Father's love and mercy:

> *Let us not forget: God never tires of forgiving us! He is the loving Father who always pardons, who has that heart of mercy for us all… God thinks like the father waiting for the son and goes to meet him; he spots him coming when he is still far off.*

When you've done something wrong, remember, your heavenly Father is waiting for you to come to him and say, "I'm sorry! Please forgive me." Spend some time talking with your parents about the beautiful gift of Confession. Perhaps you can go regularly as a family to receive this sacrament of God's mercy. In Confession you meet Jesus!

Pope Francis wants me to know that my Father in heaven will always forgive me!

14

"Jesus Gives Himself to Us in the Eucharist"

On the night before he died, Jesus celebrated the feast of the Passover with his disciples. During the meal, Jesus gave the gift of himself to his disciples in the form of bread and wine. He took a piece of unleavened bread and, looking up to heaven, he said, "This is my Body, which will be given up for you." When supper was ended, Jesus took a cup of wine and said, "This is the cup of my Blood. Do this in memory of me."

Pope Francis has an important lesson for you about the Eucharist.

Jesus makes himself a gift… He gives himself to us in the Eucharist. He shares in our journey. In Communion he gives us strength; he really helps us. He comes to us. Does a piece of bread make us so strong? Is it bread? It is not really bread. It is the Body of Jesus. Jesus comes into our hearts.

Next time you go to Mass or Eucharistic Adoration, thank Jesus for giving you the gift of himself in the Eucharist. Jesus wants to be with you on your journey to heaven. Why? Because he loves being with you! He wants to be your spiritual food to strengthen you. Jesus knows that Satan wants to tempt you to make wrong decisions. But with Jesus in your heart, you can make good choices.

Pope Francis wants me to love Jesus present in the Eucharist!

"Learn to Pray Every Day"

Jesus would often get up early and go up a mountain to talk to his Father and listen to him. His disciples knew that he was praying to his Father, but they didn't know what to do or say when they prayed. So one day when Jesus returned from praying, one of his disciples said to him, "Lord, teach us to pray." Jesus said, "When you pray say, 'Our Father in heaven, hallowed be your name…'"

Pope Francis wants to tell you about the importance of prayer:

Dear young friends, learn to pray every day: this is the way to know Jesus and invite him into your lives… He is always listening and he knows everything about us lovingly… Let's try to be open to God's word, and open to the Lord's surprises when he speaks to us.

Prayer is talking—to your heavenly Father, to Jesus, and to the Holy Spirit. You can pray the Our Father or you can just chat, anytime and anywhere.

Prayer is also letting God speak to you. He might speak to you after you receive Holy Communion, or when you are reading your Bible, or when you are just sitting quietly by yourself. You probably won't hear him with your ears, but you will hear him in your heart! Why don't you start praying—and listening to him—today.

Pope Francis wants me to pray and listen to God every day!

"Take Care of People in Need"

One day a man asked Jesus, "Who is my neighbor?" Jesus answered the question by telling a parable. There was a man who was traveling from Jerusalem to Jericho. Suddenly, robbers jumped out from behind some rocks. They beat him up, stole all of his belongings, and left him lying on the path almost dead. He needed help. But when a priest and then a Levite came by, they didn't stop to help him. Then a Samaritan came along the path. He stopped, gave the man a drink, cleansed his wounds, put him on his donkey, and took him to an inn.

Pope Francis knows that there are people everywhere who need help. Some don't have enough food or a place to live. Some are sick, disabled, lonely, or forgotten. He invites everyone to be a good neighbor. Read what he is saying to you:

Take care of people in need… If we see someone who needs help, do we stop? There is so much suffering and poverty, and a great need for good Samaritans.

It pleases Jesus so much when you take care of people in need. Every life is precious to him. Everyone is a brother or sister of Jesus. How can you or your family help someone in need?

Pope Francis wants me to remember and care for the poor!

"May I?" "Thank You" "Sorry"

Jesus was once the same age as you are now. Have you ever thought of that? He grew up in a small village called Nazareth, with Mary, his mother, and St. Joseph, his foster father. The Church calls this family "the Holy Family." Their home was loving, happy, and peaceful.

Jesus also did some of the same things that you do. He had to learn to read and write. Around his home there were chores to do, and in Joseph's workshop, Jesus learned carpentry.

Pope Francis wants us to take the Holy Family as the model for our family. He has given us some very good advice:

In our family, when we are not intrusive and ask, "May I?"; in our family, when we are not selfish and learn to say, "Thank you"; and when in a family one realizes he has done something wrong and knows how to say, "Sorry," in that family there is peace and joy. Let us remember these three words.

It's not always easy to be obedient and polite to your parents, to be thankful for all they do for you, and to ask for forgiveness when you are unkind to your brothers and sisters. Perhaps you can place these words on your refrigerator and talk about them during family meal times. And be sure to ask Mary and St. Joseph to pray for your family.

Pope Francis wants my family to be filled with peace and joy!

"Mary Is Our Mother and She Loves Us So Much"

Jesus, Mary, and his disciples were invited to a wedding in Cana. During the celebration, Mary realized there was a problem. She said, "Jesus, they have no more wine." He replied, "My hour has not yet come." But Mary said to the servants, "Do whatever he tells you."

Jesus told the servants to fill six stone jars with water. Then he said, "Pour some out and give it to the head server." The water had become wine! Mary was watching out for the bride and groom and their guests.

Pope Francis wants us to remember that Mary is also our Mother.

She is our Mother and she loves us so much. Let us allow ourselves to be watched over by her... Never forget, young friends: The Virgin Mary is our Mother, and with her help we can remain faithful to Christ.

One day when Pope Francis was speaking to the crowds, he took out a small white medicine box. Do you know what was in it? It was a rosary! He said he wasn't a pharmacist, but the fifty-nine little pills strung together were great spiritual medicine.

Do you have a rosary? It is a wonderful way to talk to Mary and to think about the life of Jesus, her Son. Perhaps a few times a week you could say a decade of the Rosary as a family for the intentions of Pope Francis.

Pope Francis wants me to know that Mary loves me!

"The Saints Are Like Us"

Paul, also called Saul, was a Pharisee. He thought he was obeying God by putting the followers of Jesus in prison. One day on the way Damascus to round up more of Jesus' followers, he was blinded by a great light. Jesus spoke to him: "Saul, Saul, why are you persecuting me?" Saul answered, "Who are you, Lord?" For three days, Saul could not see. His sight was restored when a disciple of Jesus, Ananias, prayed with him.

Pope Francis wants to encourage all of us to be saints. But just like St. Paul, who wasn't always a saint, he knows that we too can struggle to do what is right. So he gives us this lesson:

The saints are not supermen, nor were they born perfect. They are like us, like each one of us…What changed their lives? When they recognized God's love, they followed it with all their heart… Holiness is a vocation for everyone… Holiness is beautiful, it is a beautiful path!

Yes, your heavenly Father's plan for your life is for you to become a saint! It is his plan for everyone. You started on that path when you were baptized. So keep going! Don't forget to ask the Holy Spirit to help you. That's what St. Paul and all the other saints did. And be sure to to ask your favorite saint to pray for you!

Pope Francis wants me to become a saint!

26

"Be Missionaries of the Gospel"

One evening not long after Jesus' resurrection, Peter and some of his friends went fishing. Jesus was on the shore watching. He called out, "Have you caught any fish?" They answered, "No." Jesus said, "Throw your net over the other side of the boat." Immediately their net was filled with fish—so many fish that the net nearly tore!

Peter and the other disciples then became missionaries. They traveled all over the world sharing the good news about Jesus. They were no longer catching fish but catching men and women. They taught them about Jesus' life, death, and resurrection. And they brought them into the Church by baptizing them in the name of the Father, Son, and Holy Spirit.

Pope Francis knows that many people don't have a special relationship with Jesus. So he wants you to be a missionary right where you live by telling your friends and neighbors the good news of Jesus.

Dear young people, always be missionaries of the Gospel, every day and in every place… Jesus wants to be your friend and wants you to spread the joy of this friendship everywhere.

Here's how you can be a missionary. Say, "Let me tell you about my friend Jesus." Tell your friends some of the things that Jesus has done for you. Ask them if they want to read some Bible stories. And don't forget—you can be a missionary of the gospel even to grown-ups!

Pope Francis wants me to share the good news of Jesus!